Real Estate for Ambitious Beginners

How to Make Money in Real Estate and Become Your Own Boss

I0491566

Dr. Jason Hunt

Table of Contents

IMPORTANT BONUS TIP LIST!

With this book you get an extra bonus list with my Best Real Estate Investing Tips all in One Page! Things can get overwhelming especially for ambitious beginners! Refer often to this page! I've tried to pack one sheet with as much real estate wisdom as possible! To access this list please navigate to this page: http://bit.ly/2vho9XG

Introduction

I want to thank you and congratulate you for downloading the book, *"Real Estate"*.

This book has lots of actionable information on how to invest in real estate.

Real estate is perhaps one of the most stable investment vehicles out there.

Think about it; what other investment vehicle guarantees you of money at the end of the month or year and doesn't lose value year in year out because its value appreciates a lot more than the rate of inflation? What other investment vehicle can guarantee you and your family a stable income month after month even when you are directly doing very little to manage it because you have property managers? What other investment can you make money with month after month without having to follow the charts every single day to ensure you don't lose money because of occurrences that are outside your control? What other investment vehicle can you run even when you are very busy attending to other things without losing your mind?

Well, I can tell you that very few other investments out there compare to the unique benefits that come with investing in real estate. The question is; how can you invest in real estate and succeed while at it without losing your mind?

How can you deal with the problem of the huge capital outlay that's required to venture into some of the real estate investment vehicles? How can you deal with legislation to ensure you don't end up on the wrong side of the law? How do you take care of financing?

Well, this book will teach you all that and much more. In this book, you will learn what real estate is all about and how to invest in property like a pro even if you are a complete beginner in the industry. This book will show you how to invest in real estate in a way that sees you generating a profit month-in-month-out irrespective of which part of the world you choose to invest in. The book shall dissect the different types of properties and debunk real estate myths that keep many from being profitable real estate investors. As far as starting points go, few can outdo this manual.

Read on to get wiser.

Thanks again for downloading this book. I hope you enjoy it!

Dr. Jason Hunt

The trademarks that are used are without any consent, and the publication of the trademark is without permission or backing by the trademark owner. All trademarks and brands within this book are for clarifying purposes only and are the owned by the owners themselves, not affiliated with this document.

Before we get to a point of learning the specifics of investing in real estate, let's start by learning what real estate is all about.

Real Estate Investing: An Comprehensive Overview

As the title of this chapter suggests, this chapter is going to introduce you to real estate investing by discussing what is real estate investing and then detailing what qualifies you as a Real Estate investor.

Upon hearing the term real estate, most people start thinking of land, houses, or other kinds of buildings and structures. While these are huge components of what real estate is, they are only that though: components of real estate. They are in no way the complete definition of real estate.

So what exactly is real estate?

What is Real Estate?

Rather than make guesses or extrapolations to lead us to the definition of real estate, we shall go with the industry's guidebook, the USPAP's (Uniform Standards of Professional Appraisal Practice) definition.

According to USPAP, real estate is *"an identified tract or parcel of land, with the inclusion of improvements, if there are any in place"*. The term 'improvements' as used in this definition is very important in understanding real estate because essentially suggests the fact that the term real estate encompasses everything, which has been affixed permanently to the land. And this broadens the scope of what real estate entails. Improvements, as understood in the context of real estate, can include a store, home, office building, or any other structure built on the land. It can also point to anything else, which has been affixed permanently to the property. This includes things like utility systems, fences, streams, roads, grass, flowers and various trees on that land parcel.

Finally, real estate can also be inclusive of several rights that are inherent to property i.e. water rights, air and mineral rights, as well as mineral rights to any natural resources under the land.

With the all-inclusive real estate definition in place, the next step is to understand who or what a real estate investor is. **What makes one a real estate investor?**

Let's discuss that:

Well, a real estate investor is an individual, business, or other entity that invests in the real estate industry by buying, leasing, or otherwise getting the rights to a parcel of real estate or any rights that are inherent in a real estate piece.

When you look at the definition above, you begin to understand why real estate is such a wide field and why there exists many kinds of real estate investing.

Investing in real estate will often consist of the investment categories most people immediately think of when they hear the term. This includes things like owning commercial and residential property and renting the property out, or buying such property to quickly improve and resell for a profit. However, it can also refer to lots of other investment opportunities, with the inclusion of buying and then leasing of mineral rights to a land parcel. This is where this guide comes in to simplify the seemingly complex topic:

Getting Started In Real Estate Investing

Real estate investing is one of those terms aptly named 'umbrella terms', in that it encompasses several lines of action. Insofar as investing goes, it encompasses property renting, house flipping, property wholesaling, and a lot more. You also have the option of either investing in commercial property or residential real estate. It is up to you to decide what works for you.

As far as investment properties go, you have a wide range of variety. This is inclusive of multi-family apartment homes, single-family homes, retail space, condominiums, college rentals, office buildings, and much more. When you are just getting started in the field, it is very likely that you have spent more than a few hours worrying about what kind of property best suits you. It is also likely that you have spent a lot of time wondering what real estate investing is all about so you can plan your actions around that.

To put it simply, when you invest in real estate, your goal will be to put in money today and get it to work, and give it a chance to increase so that in the future, you have more money. The return or profit you make should be enough to cover the risk you take when you invest in real estate, taxes you need to pay, and the costs of owning the investment such as regular maintenance, utilities, and insurance costs.

When you understand the basic investment factors, risks, and economics of the field, it is easier to succeed by making calculated steps.

In a nutshell, to win at real estate investing, you need to fulfill the following:

1. Successfully buy property

2. Avoid bankruptcy while you are at it

3. Generate rent or sales that allow you to purchase even more properties

This is quite simple, is it not? It actually is quite simple. However, remember that simple does not always mean easy especially in this particular field. If you make mistakes, you could lose everything and end up bankrupt.

Now that you understand how you can invest, what are some of the real estate investments you can make as an investor?

Where Can You Invest? The Real Estate Investment Options

There exists multiple ways through which you can make money from real estate. Some seasoned real estate experts have come out to say that rental properties fit the 'real estate investment' term better than everything else does. Others have disputed this and even perhaps downplayed rental properties. The truth however, is that all real estate investments that generate an income qualify 100% as investment ventures.

Below are common ways through which you can invest your money in real estate as a beginner.

1: Rental properties

Rental properties operate on the basic idea that you make money via **cash flow** and **appreciation**.

Cash flow will be the money you make from incoming rent. Take note that you should only consider this amount after paying off all expenses. Expenses may include tax, maintenance allowances, insurance, HOA dues, vacancies, and mortgage payments.

If you manage to buy rentals below market value, which is a massive advantage for you by the way, it is possible to make money soon after purchasing a property. You may also buy a property that needs work done on it or has suffered from consistent poor management and can shine after quick renovations.

Appreciation occurs when market values move up, as they are bound to with time. Appreciation will provide a nice bonus for you and may bump up profits significantly.

However, understand that it is not all roses here. Not every market will be ideal for rentals. Often times, the more expensive the housing market, the harder it will be to invest in rentals.

There are different types of rental units that you can invest in some of which include the following:

- ***Multi-family apartments***

Whether you choose to flip these or make them into rentals, you are bound to turn a profit.

A multifamily unit refers to any property that has two or more units. A multifamily unit could be a duplex where you own the two sides of it, or a 400-unit apartment building. Multifamily units are great in that they can greatly reduce maintenance costs.

The good thing with these is that if your rental property has several units, the likelihood of having every unit vacant is low, which means you will always see some revenues streaming in even if they are not so much (investing in a single family unit for renting it out is not exactly a very good investment plan; the best you can do is to rent it out on part time basis e.g. using AirBnb for instance. However, they can also have higher utility, maintenance, and vacancy costs.

- ***College rentals***

These can be single-family properties, multifamily apartments, or condominiums. The common characteristic is that their ideal tenants are college students. While they can produce higher rental figures, the maintenance costs are often quite high as well.

- ***Vacation homes***

On paper, vacation rentals look phenomenal because you get to rent them out for lofty figures each day, week, or month. However, seasons can and will play a huge role in the rental income amount you can realize. Management fees will also be higher than the typical rental.

2: House Flipping

Flipping houses operates on a very simple concept: you buy a house, fix it up so that it is all-pretty, and then sell it off for a profit. As mentioned earlier in this book, simple does not necessarily mean easy; executing a successful flip is usually tough business. You will need to consider many expenses such as carrying costs (HOA fees, taxes, insurance, and utilities), financing costs, buying costs, and selling costs.

A lot of the time, beginners will believe that repairs will constitute all or most of the cost. This is wrong, as repairs are only part of the cost. Other costs include financing costs, selling costs, buying costs etc.

Repair costs can include fixing up broken windows by investing in new window frames and panes, giving the house a new coat of paint in the case of peeling paint, replacing the ceiling, replacing worn or soiled carpets, fixing broken toilets, repairing broken door handles and knobs, and the likes.

The thing is; today, the competition for flips is intense. However, do not let this put you off: you can find deals via auctions, MLS, for-sale-by-owners, wholesalers and via directly marketing yourself.

Examples of property you can flip as a beginner:

- *Single family homes*

Also called SFRs in the real estate circles, SFRs can be attached or detached. A good example of an attached home is a duplex side while an example of a detached SFR is a stand-alone house.

SFRs will be easier to get financing for and will be easier to buy owing to greater inventory. They are also easy to sell since you have a consumer group that includes both owner-occupants and investors looking for such property. If you fancy, you can hold off on selling SFRs and instead use them as rental income sources. The best part about this investment vehicle is that you will rarely have to employ real estate management companies to manage them properly since you can deal with tenants directly. Moreover, tenants tend to live in many SFRs for quite long, which means you are more or less guaranteed long-term rental income from such tenants. That's not all; many tenants in SFRs are likely to show lots of respect and will handle most of the utilities.

- ***Townhouses or condos***

These will usually be part of a complex but possessing many similarities to single-family homes. Often times, the complex will have a homeowners association that will handle part of the property and may go even further and pay for some utilities.

Townhouses and condos will have attached neighbors. They are very decent investments but you will need to watch out for HOA fees. They also have the characteristic of appreciating far more slowly than the typical single family home.

3: Real Estate Wholesaling

This is when an investor buys a house, gets it under contract but rather than keeping it or fixing it up so he can flip it at a later time, simply goes ahead and sells it to another investor.

It is quite possible to wholesale properties without using your own money. One way you can do this is by getting the house under contract and then assigning that contract to another investor who will actually buy that house. Yet another way is to utilize the 'double close'. The first investor will buy the property on the same day they sell it to a different investor.

The thing is; as with everything else, real estate wholesaling is not easy to pull off despite the simplicity of the concept it operates on.

So where exactly should you start? Here is a power tip that will help you to make an informed decision:

Pro Tip: The easiest properties to understand are residential single-family homes. They are also the easiest to buy and sell as they provide far fewer hoops. When you are just getting started in real estate investing, the simplest route is to begin by investing in singular family homes and advancing to projects that require patience and expertise. Still, it will not hurt to understand what various real estate investment projects are about, as we've discussed.

The question you might be having right now is; through real estate investments such as those covered above, how do you, a real estate investor, generate income from your investments?

Where The Money Is In Real Estate

Here are some of the ways:

1. Real estate appreciation: This happens when your property's value increases because of changes in the real estate market. It could be that the land around your property becomes scarcer or just busier such as when developers build a major mall a few meters away.

2. Cash flow income: You make cash flow income off real estate if you rent it out to tenants who then pay you rent/lease at agreed times.

3. Real estate related income: This is the sort of income 'specialists' (think of brokers, real estate management companies and such parties) in the game earn. They will make money from commissions from sales or from collecting a percentage from the rental figures for running daily operations.

4. Ancillary real estate investment income: For some investments, this may present a huge profit source. By ancillary investments, we mean things such as vending machines in offices, laundry facilities in apartment buildings, and the likes.

With that comprehensive understanding of the concept of real estate, let's now understand how you stand to gain by investing in real estate.

How Do You Stand To Gain By Investing In Real Estate?

In truth, no investment in the world can give you a 100% profit guarantee or even a 100% principal protection guarantee. Anybody that tells you otherwise is a liar or likely knows very little about investing. However, throughout history, real estate has proven itself as one of those asset classes that is safest in that it hardly brings about major losses, is always appreciating and brings about many other direct and indirect benefits.

That's not all; investing in real estate opens you up to several possible benefits that are hard to come by with most other asset classes.

Here are a few of these benefits.

1: Investing In Real Estate Gives You Control

Another real estate aspect investors find valuable is the elevated control they enjoy over their investments. What do we mean by this?

Look at investments such as stock and bond investments. When you invest in stocks, the next step is passively waiting until the stocks increase in value. Unless you happen to be a major shareholder in the company you invested in, you will have very little say on operations that can improve your stock value. The only time you will feel like you have some control is during annual general meetings when they allow you to ask a question or two.

Compare this to investing in real estate. When you invest in real estate, you enjoy a degree of control over every relative variable. Whatever profits you aim to generate will rely on your negotiation skills: you can dedicate yourself to acquiring as much knowledge as you can on real estate, find creative ways to make additional revenue, and much more.

2: You Can Enjoy Leverage As A Real Estate Investor

Real estate offers you the opportunity to leverage your capital several times over. Let us break this down so you can understand it better:

Real estate investors may use borrowed funds to invest in a real estate piece they could otherwise not afford outright and still realize the full profit potential from ownership of that particular property. However, understand that it is not always as simple as it looks. With increased leverage comes an increased degree of risk. Keep this in mind at all times.

3: Real Estate Offers A Wide Array Of Tax Advantages

Did you know that real estate could offer tax benefits often unavailable to other investors? For instance, most governments classify real estate profits as capital gains. Capital gains have lower taxation than employment income.

In addition, the tax basis of your investment can decrease as time goes by as the tax code allows you to depreciate real estate every year. The other thing is that if you are making money from a rental property unit, this essentially means you can as well enjoy all the money without worrying about self-employment taxation.

Let's now start the journey to investing in real estate starting with understanding how you can actually invest in real estate even when you don't have a lot of money.

The Cost of Investing in Real Estate

Is it possible to invest in real estate with little or no money? If so, how can you start investing in real estate with little to no money?

Most new real estate investors do not have a limitless supply of money to invest in real estate. If this is your case, do not worry much because there are lots of others like you who are interested in real estate investment but have to pace their expenditure.

While this book intends to open our eyes so you can see possibilities where you previously saw none, it will not insult your intelligence as so many motivational manuals often do. Without money, or with a small amount of it, buying property will be tough. It is, however, not impossible; there will always be something you can do to improve your situation. It is possible to invest in real estate with no money but it will take a lot of work.

Here are some ways you can invest with little money:

1: Purchasing As an Owner-Occupant

If you want to buy rentals or flip houses with no money, the best way to go about it is to purchase as an owner-occupant. You will live in this house for a year, maybe two, and then make a sale or rent the house out. While it takes some money to buy a house as an owner-occupant, it will cost you very little compared to dealing with investor loans.

Earlier, we mentioned something about private money and borrowing from lenders. Since this is a good way to go if your credit rating is high, are well connected or cannot raise the required amount to acquire a certain property, you may need external financing. Let's discuss financing in the next part.

2: Getting Into Partnerships with Other Investors

In the real estate investing scene, you will find partners who are open to getting into partnerships with rental property owners or flippers such as yourself. You may be asking yourself, "Why don't these people go ahead and invest directly rather than having to go through other real estate investors?" The answer is that they may lack the time or patience to scour through properties, wait until they find the best deals, nor have the contacts to get them the best deals in the shortest time possible. What they have at their disposal is the money and the intent to make even more of it from real estate. This is where you come in.

You will do the legwork: it is up to you to find great deals and your partner investor will provide the financing to buy and flip the properties. In some cases, these partners will provide 100% of the money. While they are certainly available, they are quite hard to find. The challenge though is that most of the time, they will prefer to work with established operators with a sizable portfolio as opposed to working with newbies.

3: Using Private Money

Private money is an option if you are having a hard time financing your venture or cannot come up with 20% down to buy a house via mortgage. Private money will come from private lenders (think more along the lines of Shakespeare's 'Shylock') who will usually attach very high interest rates. Private money is great, especially since there are no stipulations such as the '20% down' one. However, you need to be wise here since there is no person on Facebook, or some mysterious site that will offer you 100% of a deal at an interest rate of 3% (these scams are all over the web and especially Facebook).

4: Buying Houses 'Subject To a Loan'

Here, you target houses that have loans on them. Think of a house whose mortgage is yet fully paid. With a very small amount of money, you can buy a house that has a loan on it. The reason for this, as you may have already figured out, is that the owner does not fully own it since there is mortgage payments that still needs clearing. However, most of the time, these houses do not present good deals let alone great ones.

It is also possible the bank could call the loan due at any time. However, when such a deal works, it can set your investing career up and help you move on to better and luxurious deals.

5: Wholesaling

We briefly touched on this by saying that this is when, rather than purchasing a house outright, an investor gets it under contract (or purchases its 'selling rights') at a fee. The investor will agree with the original seller on a fixed figure that the seller expects to get back from the sale. The wholesaler, rather than keeping it or fixing it up so he can flip it at a later time, simply goes ahead and sells it to another investor at a higher price than agreed with the original seller. He will then pocket the extra amount (he keeps this as a finder's fee.)

This is the most common method taught to real estate investors who want to invest but have limited reserves. You will make money from wholesaling, even large amounts of it, but you will need to have some money nonetheless. The cheapest wholesaling method is the well-known **'driving for dollars'.** Driving for dollars means exactly that: armed with a phone, you will hop into your car and drive around looking for property after which you pitch for the contract idea to prospective sellers (you need to have a prospective buyer in mind by then) then get in touch with the prospective buyer who you then sell the house to at whatever price you feel is fit for you. A couple hundred dollars is enough to get you started.

Financing Your Real Estate Investment: The Options

As far as real estate investing is concerned, you can follow either of several options including using your own money (savings), private money lenders, hard money lenders, crowd funding and many others. In this chapter, we will discuss private money lenders, hard money lenders and crowd funding.

Private Money Lenders Vs. Hard Money Lenders

One of the greatest features of real estate is that unlike investing in places like stock where you cannot afford to gamble with borrowed funds to buy stock, you can comfortably invest in real estate with borrowed money and succeed while at it. In fact, many of the real estate properties out there are financed through debt!

More precisely, there will be loans available if what you are interested in are rentals. There are loans available if you want to major in house flipping. What you should understand is that these loans differ from each other. Loans on property for rent are often very similar to owner occupant loans that have terms that can go for as long as 30 years. However, you can expect a bit higher interest rates.

When flipping houses, the loans will be different. Banks hate loan money paid back right away since they like their interest money. For flipper loans, the term is usually a year or less and the interest rates are a lot higher. The best way to finance these is using private money lenders although bank loans are still okay.

With this in mind, let us look at private money lenders and hard money lenders and how to find them.

>Using Private Lenders To Finance Your Real Estate Investment

Who is a private lender?

It is necessary to understand who a private lender is and what differentiates him or her from a hard money lender. Have you tried looking for private money lenders on Google? You likely came across a slew of results, right? At least 95% of the companies that popped up are not private money lenders; the latter are difficult to reach via Google.

A hard money lender, such as most of those companies that popped up, specializes in borrowing money from investors and immediately lending it to house flippers at much higher rates. The rates on hard money are often absurd-: they can climb up to 20%.

A true private money lender is one who has a lot of personal cash on hand and is willing to lend it directly to different individual investors as opposed to using hard money lenders. Private money can also come from friends, family, or business partners.

Why Is A Private Lender Vital To Flipping Homes?

This will only require a couple of sentences to explain.

In case you do not know it, truly succeeding at flipping houses hinges on one thing: volume. The more houses you are flipping at a given time, the higher your success rate. If you major on flipping, you have little choice but to look to flip several houses at a time. This is only possible if you have a lot of financing in place. Private money lenders will greatly help you out on this.

How Can You Find A Private Money Lender?

Before you even think of using private money to finance your real estate investment, you should appreciate the possible roadblocks to accessing private money so that you can overcome them.

Here are the most common roadblocks to accessing private money:

1. Investors have very little experience in flipping houses, and private lenders are unwilling to take risks on them.

2. Investors are unwilling to ask family or friends because they are scared of losing the money as well as scared of being turned down

3. Investors barely know people with a lot of cash who could double up as private money lenders

How to Overcome These Obstacles

1. If you have little experience flipping houses, the only cure to this is to gain experience. Ease your way into it via wholesaling and steadily round out your portfolio.

2. If you do not know of people with money to spare, there are ways to get to know such people. Make a list of everyone you know, or may have connections with, who may have sufficient money.

3. If you are scared of rejection, real estate is not for you. In real estate, rejection happens at such a high frequency that it is almost impossible to avoid. As for being afraid of losing

the money of people you know, should you not be more afraid of losing the money of people you do not know?

>Using Hard Money Lenders To Finance Your Real Estate Investment

Finding a hard money lender is quite easy: a simple Google search on hard money lenders will easily turn up over 1 million results. The tough bit is finding a hard money lender whose rates make sense, has a record of investing in your local market, and has experience. Most hard money lenders will charge interest rates of 15% and above and many more will be toothless when a deal is on the line. The trouble with most hard money lenders is that you cannot trust them not to drop the ball at the most tender of moments.

So how exactly do hard money loans work? Here is how:

How Hard Money Loans Work

These are not loans from a bank and as such, you cannot expect them to work in a similar manner. In hard money situations, the hard money lender will borrow money from investors and then lend that same money to other investors looking to buy real estate. He or she will attach higher interest rates to the loan as a way to turn a profit.

A typical hard money lender will see rates in the 15%-18% range, plus an additional charge of 2 to 5 points on the loan. To explain this further, a 5 point fee on a loan of $100,000 will be $5,000.

If you don't have any problem with the rates, I know you might be wondering; so how can you find a good hard money lender?

How to Find a Good Hard Money Lender

While many small hard money lenders will attach lofty interest rates to their loans, larger lending companies now coming into the scene have reasonable interest rates. The reason they can do this is that instead of getting their money from multiple small investors, they get their money from large sized hedge funds who do not demand as high a return as the smaller investor. Many large hard money lenders will have interest rates as low as 11% with 2-3 points on the loan.

Here are a couple of good, nationwide hard money lenders:

Fund that Flip

Lima Capital Hard Money

Then the next question you might have is; can you find good hard money lenders in your locality? The answer is a 'yes'; here is how to go about it:

How to Find a Local Hard Money Lender

If you prefer working with a local lender, be extremely careful of whom you deal with. Here are a few ways to find local hard money lenders:

1. Ask around at local real estate investor meet-ups

2. Ask your real estate agents if they know of any hard money lenders

3. Check with online real estate investor communities.

The other option you can choose to finance your real estate investment venture is to use crowdfunding. Let's discuss how to go about it next.

Using Crowd Funding To Finance Your Real Estate Investment

What is real estate crowd funding?

Real estate crowd funding entails pooling funds from many people with each person contributing a small portion of a certain amount towards a certain goal. With the growth of the internet, crowd funding takes place through different internet based platforms these days. In this case, as a real estate investor, you pitch your investment idea to prospective investors on different crowd funding platforms then sit back to wait for money to come in from investors all over the world. The investors in this case are people who believe in your business idea and want to help you to get it off the ground while of course expecting some returns on investment.

The good thing about crowd funding is that you can be on either side and still be considered a real estate investor. For instance, you can be on the crowd funding platforms to raise money to finance your real estate investment endeavors or you can be on the crowd funding platform as an investor i.e. one of those who advance money to direct investors in real estate. In this case, all you do is to source for financing, advance it to borrowers through the crowd funding platforms then sit back to wait for your return on investment.

Crowd funding comes with a twist:

The real estate businesses that need capital may structure their investment opportunities as debt or equity financing. This means investors who are researching real estate crowd funding opportunities can come across deals that offer them either equity investments where they may participate in the upside profit on a real estate deal or debt-based investments (paid back

33

with interest in specified installments or at the end of a certain period).

Even though crowd funding is still quite new, it is already a multi-billion dollar industry. In fact, it is very usual for a typical crowd-funding platform to have invested upwards of $250 million. This makes it a great way to raise money as well as invest.

I know you might be wondering whether crowd funding is a safer investment.

Is Crowd Funding The Safest Way To Invest In Real Estate?

Well, the truth is; no investment has a sure guarantee: all types of investments, including real estate crowd funding, have a risk rider. However, sophisticated platforms of crowd funding thoroughly review every real estate deal and the team behind it before they make it available as an option to investors on their site.

In addition, the opportunities offered on the crowd funding platforms offer the general comfort of making your investment in a physical property piece as opposed to a bond or stock or any other non-physical asset.

Now that you understand how to go about it as a beginner and how to raise the needed financing to get started, the next chapter will focus on setting the right systems to protect yourself.

Protection for Real Estate Investors: A How to Guide

In this chapter, we shall seek look at the how to protect yourself as you invest in real estate with the best option being opting to form a LLC. Let's discuss that briefly:

Understanding LLC

A LLC, or Limited Liability Company, can be a powerful tool of protection against liabilities on properties, especially rental properties. This is so important that some real estate investors set up separate LLCs for each individual property they own. LLCs let you privately own property and assets deemed hard to trace if liabilities come up. With LLCs, your will register your property in the name of the LLC, as opposed to your own, thus effectively eliminating it as a target in the case of (the quite common) property lawsuits and resulting fee penalties.

What Should Compel You To Put Your Property In A LLC?

To put it bluntly, owning property has a substantial liability risk. When it comes to rental properties, this risk considerably multiplies. The thing with owning property is that at any time, somebody can sue you personally or aggressively attack your assets via the courtroom. You do not even have to have done anything to provoke a reaction. A flawed assessment here and a hasty conclusion there is enough to convince somebody to sue you. If you own your property in a LLC, with a separate checking account in place, there is a good chance that the lawsuit shall only affect the property in question.

How Difficult Is It To Put Your Rental Property In A LLC?

There is no straightforward answer to this one: it will depend on your particular state. In Colorado, creating an LLC is quite easy; all you need to adhere to is a two-step plan: create the necessary paperwork, and have the documents submitted to the Secretary of State. Unless your circumstances are incredibly unique, you will most likely have it approved. Different state will have different requirements in place. Some states, like the aforementioned Colorado, will make your process very easy. Others will have you jump through a few hoops.

However, have this in mind: you do not have to register a LLC in your resident state. You can register your LLC in any state you want without any complications. If you register it in a state different from your home state, you will not have the taxman or other authorities giving you a hard time. It also costs next to nothing to create and register one. Speaking of costs:

How Much Will It Cost to set up a LLC?

We will stick to using Colorado as an example. In Colorado, it costs $50, if you create your documents and file them in person, which is not hard at all. Every year, you will pay a $10 filing fee to keep the LLC active. Other states may charge a lesser or bigger amount.

The bottom line here is that you cannot go wrong with an LLC. In fact, with what's at stake if anything were to go wrong, you should be thinking of registering one as soon as you can. They cost very little to set up, provide sufficient protection for your assets, and best of all, no court can compel you to divulge your different LLC owned properties if you choose not to.

Next, we will discuss how to deal with risks as a real estate investor.

Dealing With Risks

In truth, real estate investing is risky and this is understandable because in any case, what worthwhile investment is risk free? Nonetheless, if you do things right, you will discover that real estate investing is not as risky as your naysaying friends want you to think. You should also consider this: over 50% of all those steering you away from it have never invested in it.

So how exactly do you deal with risks? Here are some ideas on how to go about it:

How to Mitigate Real Estate Investment Risk

What can you do to mitigate real estate investment risks? Here are some steps to take:

1: Invest For Cash Flow

Cash flow should be the most important factor in your real estate strategy, especially if you want it to be around long. This is why it makes a lot of sense to invest in rentals. Sure enough, you have to deal with all sorts of tenants and have to enlist a real estate management company for a percentage of your returns; even so, you cannot deny the capacity of rentals to uphold the cash flow factor. Come rain or shine, as long as you do things properly, you will have consistent cash flowing in.

Let us shed more light on this:

If you invest in a good property, not necessarily a spectacular one, but one with reasonable standards, and fix it up to raise its standard, you can expect at least $500 in cash flow a month. It is also likely that you will receive more than this: perhaps up to $800 if you provide proper amenities.

With cash flow of $700 to $800 a month for a couple of units, your rent will range from $1300 to $1600. To have negative cash flow, your rent would have to drop by a full 50%, which is very unlikely. Sure enough, it is possible that house prices could fall by 50%, but when you consider that the highest drop was by 40%, and this was during the infamous house crash almost a decade ago, you begin to see why chances for this are slim.

2: Be Wise in Your Choice of Property Investment

Choose the types of properties you invest in wisely: this has a say in how much of a risk you incur.

This book will give you a straightforward suggestion: as a beginner, focus on single-family properties that are less than 50 years old. These provide the lowest risk for you and are often very easy to sell off.

3: Purchase Property below Market Value

One key thing to a low risk real estate investment strategy is to buy property below market value. The argument behind this is straightforward: by purchasing below market value, you create instant equity, raise your net worth, and stay protected against market downturns. Speaking of the latter, while the real estate market will never have the turbulence of an investment option such as the stock market, like every other investment field, it is still susceptible to downturns.

To make it even easier to succeed, the next chapter will give you tips that will put you on the path to success as far as investing in real estate is concerned.

Easing You In: Valuable Knowledge & Tips for Novice Investors

Here are several tips that will prove valuable to you in your journey to become a seasoned real estate investor.

1. Be Financially Fit

Before you invest in rental properties, buff up your financial fitness: Pay close attention to your monthly budget and make sure your insurance coverage is adequate. Many successful real estate investors use their savings to build their investment portfolio and then steadily buying property. You can consider this route.

2. Establish Good Credit

Never underestimate the role of having a good credit standing because the best real estate returns rely upon credit use to obtain leverage to use other people's money.

3. Go for small apartment buildings & single family homes

Among residential property options, the top recommendations are the small apartment buildings & single-family homes. We mentioned this at an earlier part of this book. Let us discuss it a bit more deeply. Attached houses make a lot of sense for the investor who does not want to deal with issues such as building maintenance and security. It is also true that as far as prices go, attached housing tends to perform best in the developed urban environments.

4. Rental Property Niche Is a Fickle Mistress

The thing is, although countless people have succeeded by investing in rental properties, the sad truth is that the rental property niche is not for everyone

Before you make an investment, it is important to consider your current investment preferences as well as your personal temperament before you buy property. Do you have the patience to handle tenants in a rental property? Are you in your zone when troubleshooting problems or when hiring a property manager? Ask yourself these questions before you make a move.

5. Make Residential Properties Your Priority

In the beginning, focus on residential property because as a beginner real estate investor, there is likely a lot that you do not know about real estate investing that investing in commercial real estate could be too much for you. Your first steps need to be smart. In comparison to most other property types, residential property is an attractive investment that is easy to understand, buy, and manage.

6. Buy a Home to Live in

Your first (and usually one of the very best) real estate investment will be to buy a home to live in. Real estate investment is the only investment we know that allows you to live in, or rent out to provide income. It is also possible to derive large tax-free profits upon selling your home at a much higher price than how much you paid at the time of purchase.

Conclusion

We have come to the end of the book. Thank you for reading and congratulations for reading until the end.

Sometimes, real estate investing, especially to the beginner, may seem intimidating. It is very easy to feel as if this is something only pros are able to do. I hope this book was simple enough to help you fast-track your journey to becoming a seasoned real estate investor.

It is true that this book does not contain 100% of everything you need to know as a real estate investor: no book does. However, it covers the most important points you need to be familiar with when getting started.

If you found the book valuable, can you recommend it to others? One way to do that is to post a review on Amazon.

Thank you and good luck!

Also, don't forget to download my bonus tip list! Go to this page:

http://bit.ly/2vho9XG

Dr. Jason Hunt